C0-BWX-337

WORDS FOR THE JOURNEY

The Chrysalis Group Presents a
Collection of Reflections

Edited by
Liz Whitehurst
Susan Wilkes

To Jenny
Susan

WORDS FOR THE JOURNEY: Copyright 2012 by The Chrysalis Group, Inc.

All rights reserved including the right to reproduce this book or portions thereof in any form whatsoever. All writing and images are the property of the artists.

Designed by Trina Lambert / www.trinadlambert.com

Cover photo: *Iona*. Margaret Woodson Nea
Back Cover photo: *Labyrinth*. B Millner

B Millner

Boat House. A view from the Millners' cottage on LaGrange Creek, where Nancy did much of her writing.

Nancy Bost Millner
(1939-2007)

Founder and first president of The Chrysalis Group.

Teacher, guide, dreamer, community leader, wife, visionary, friend, counselor, mother, spiritual seeker, grandmother, companion to many, inspiration to all.

Meaning

Spiritual Practices

Creativity

Inner Work

Mindfulness

Artists

Priscilla Burbank – 39, *Sea Whimsies.*

Jason Hill – 9, *Call Forth the Moon*, Angor Temple complex, Siem Reap, Cambodia; 56, *Paradise Pool*, Phuket, Thailand; 67, *The Coming Storm*, Angor Wat temple, Siem Reap, Cambodia.

Adrian Luxmoore – 28, *Risen.* This silver chalice was a part of Nancy Millner's chalice collection, a gift from her husband, B.

Kathleen McSweeney – 1, *Celtic Stone,* Midlothian, Virginia; 6, *Bright Leaves,* Richmond, Virginia; 51, *Walking In,* Fort Popham, Maine; 76, *Perspective,* Grand Traverse County, Michigan.

B Millner – Dedication page, *Boat House*; 17, *Pete's Boat*; 43, *Red Buoy;* 72, *Mudscape*; 80, *Anne Ascending.* This sculpture was Nancy Millner's favorite. Back cover, *Labyrinth.*

Margaret Woodson Nea – Front cover, *Cairn*, West Beach, Iona; 2, *Candlelight*, Abbey Iona; 12, *Double Rainbow*, Iona; 18, *Deep Peace, Running Wave*, Iona; 21, *Spirit of Trees*, Canada; 24, *Found Labyrinth*, North Beach, Iona; 33, *Island in Mist*, Maine; 35, *Sunrise over Mull*, Scotland; 48, *Raindrop*, Pine Needle, Virginia; 52, *Tapestry of Trees*, North Carolina; 60, *Seashore*, North Beach, Iona; 63, *Dahlia,* Maine; 68, *Mountain Stream*, Appalachia.

> " Wise words, our own and/or those of
> others, can teach us what we do not yet know.
> We can use words to communicate with, and
> give expression to, our incomplete inner selves. "
>
> – Nancy Bost Millner, *Words for the Journey*, "First Words"

The monthly e-publication *Words for the Journey* was born around the kitchen table of Nancy Millner, the late founder of The Chrysalis Group. Nancy's uncanny ability to see an idea as though it were already reality and her willingness to expend energy to bring it to fruition brought us to this moment around her table. I love the memory because it captures that quintessential aspect of Nancy, and because it also reminds me of her generosity of spirit. She had invited four Chrysalis Board members who were interested in writing to visit with her in her home about the project.

As she ushered us into her kitchen, afternoon sun streamed through the many windows overlooking her garden. Birdsong accompanied us as we enjoyed the tea, brie and crackers, fruit and sweets she had prepared. Plans for the publication flowed easily and as we drew to an end, the ever-organized Nancy pulled out her old-school calendar — no electronic devices for Nancy! Hands flipping open the worn leather edges, she lifted her pen and eagerly asked when we should schedule the next meeting. Someone questioned whether we really needed to have another meeting. Earlier in her life, she might have persuaded us to gather again for further planning. This time, Nancy paused and smiled with soft eyes. Her hands relaxed as she said in her gentle Southern voice, "No, I guess not, except to love each other."

Words for the Journey was thus born out of vision and love. The publication reflects Nancy's commitment to dual purposes of doing her inner work and aiding other seekers in pursuing their own journeys. Nancy once told me that whenever I had a powerful spiritual experience, I must write about it. We were leaving a meeting and I had made a casual comment about an awakening I experienced. I was struck at the time by the conviction in her voice, especially in response to a brief remark.

To be honest, in my younger, more willful days, I sometimes found myself resisting Nancy's shared wisdom, but I was also familiar with the stunning clarity of her insight. Her mandate to write resonated with what she referred to as "clear knowing." "I will, Nancy," I replied. She had illuminated the powerful pathway writing can be for coming into contact with our own deeper knowing and for expansion of the soul. True to Nancy's understanding of the spiritual journey, *Words for the Journey* was designed to both share the written wisdom of Chrysalis members as well as encourage readers to "use words to communicate with, and give expression to, our incomplete inner selves."

Nancy wrote the first *Words for the Journey* piece in October, 2004 and Chrysalis has continued to publish reflections each month since then. In many of her endeavors, Nancy's mission was to support people in exploring the spiritual side of life and to assure us that we are all part of a Larger Story, a Greater Reality. All of the authors who have written for *Words for the Journey* since the beginning are represented in this volume. As members of Chrysalis continue to expand upon and interpret Nancy's original vision for a new audience, we are pleased to make this selection of reflections available to a wider community.

– Susan Brock Wilkes, Fall 2012

" Perhaps we write – and read – toward what we will become. May it be so for all of us. "

- Nancy Bost Millner, *Creative Aging*

Meaning

First Words

by Nancy Bost Millner

MW Nea

66 Oh bless the continuous stutter
of the Word being made into flesh. 99
– Leonard Cohen

I have always loved words, but only recently have I come to see my attraction to words as a contemplative practice. Perhaps, by making too many demands that they immediately offer information, I have not given words the time and respect they deserve as they "stutter into flesh." Words can do more than give information. They can expand our souls. Perhaps anything to which we are deeply attracted and to which we give sincere, focused attention can expand our souls.

Coleman Barks, major translator of the work of Sufi poet Rumi, tells the story of a man in prison who was sent a prayer rug by a friend. The prisoner had wanted a crowbar or a key to escape, but as he began using the prayer rug, bowing, sitting up, bowing again, he noticed an odd design in the weaving of the rug.

The design was exactly where his head would touch the rug as he prayed. As he focused his attention on the weaving, he discovered there the pattern for the lock that confined him to prison and he was able to escape and set himself free.

Words, whether our own or those of others, which are sincerely chosen and consistently meditated upon, may set us free also. Some of these freeing words tiptoe softly — even silently — into our consciousness while others march in to the sound of booming drums. Perhaps words know how loudly they must speak to inspire, inform and grace our lives. Inspired words can connect heart, mind and body. Without heart, words are often dry. Without mind, words may fail to communicate to others the highly personal truth of the heart. With heart and mind, words can move our bodies to tears, laughter or shivers of sudden acknowledgment that truth is present.

Graceful words can make our hearts sing. They can charm with their rhythm and their sound so that their fragrance, like that of a stargazer lily, stops us in our tracks and momentarily transports us into another realm. They can also inspire us — sometimes for a lifetime. How many of us can recall a sentence that changed our direction, our understanding or our relationship with someone?

Wise words, our own and/or those of others, can teach us what we do not yet know. We can use words to communicate with, and give expression to, our incomplete inner selves. We can use words to dialogue with the wisdom of the ages and with people whom we will never meet. Like May Sarton, I have never happily engaged in a long writing assignment without the motivation to learn something I did not already know. In our stuttering, we often move a bit closer to knowing what we did not know we knew.

66 I have written every poem, every novel, for the same purpose — to find out what I think, to know where I stand. 99 – May Sarton

Contemplation of words can act as prayer as they draw us into our authentic selves and beyond our individual selves — as they connect our personal stories to a Larger Story of which we are all a part. May we journey long enough for the words of our lives to find their melody.

Journey Suggestions

Obtain a beautiful journal, a special pen and start collecting and recording quotations that attract you. Each week select a quotation that especially speaks to you.

Pause and give your selected quotation sincere, focused attention.

As thoughts and feelings arise, dialogue in your journal with the words you have chosen. You might dialogue about why you chose these words and/or how they connect with your life at this time.

Nancy Bost Millner was the founder of The Chrysalis Group. She initiated the monthly *Words for the Journey* reflections in 2004.

Surprised by Joy

by Joan Garrabrant

I am frequently reminded of Carl Jung's words, "That which crosses my willful path I call God." On a recent Thursday morning around eight a.m., God crossed my path on Cardwell Road in Goochland County. It was a typical school/ work day morning. I was responsibly taking my granddaughter to school before I went on to work. I was driving along thinking responsible thoughts about the day ahead: the groceries to be bought, the bills to be paid, the school projects to be checked up on, the reports to be written, when up ahead, right in the path of my car, sat God, wagging his fluffy white tail and looking pleased with himself and the world around him. Of course, I didn't recognize God at first. At the time he seemed to be a tan and white puppy with soft, soft fur and a deep sense that all was right with the world.

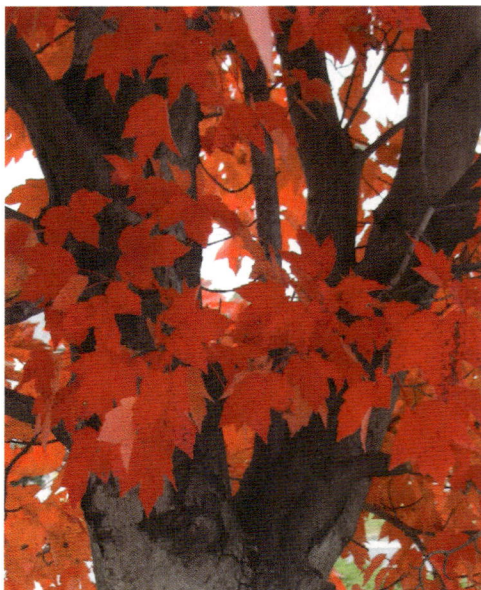
Kathleen McSweeney

66 If one completes the journey to one's own heart, one will find oneself in the heart of everyone else. 99 – Father Thomas Keating

I hastily stopped the car, and with cars piling up behind me, got out and encouraged him to move to the field by the side of the road to better survey the wonders of creation. He looked at me quizzically and seemed to agree, but then decided the view from under my car was vastly preferable. Horns began to blow behind me and I knew we were delaying an increasing number of folks from continuing along their willful paths. I was finally able to convince him that a ride in the car might be fun and my granddaughter, God, and I took off down the road much to the relief of those behind me.

After taking my granddaughter to school, I returned home to begin trying to locate the owner. I was a little concerned that Jimmy, our two-year-old collie mix, might feel less than pleased at the sudden appearance of this newcomer and I gave him a dog biscuit to reassure him. Jimmy took the dog biscuit from my hand and went over to the puppy and gently dropped it at his feet. It was then that the first conscious recognition that this was no ordinary puppy hit. As fate would have it, we were unable to find the owner, although we did try, hoping all the while that we would be unsuccessful. And thus Toby joined our family.

When I first encountered him, I knew I couldn't help but smile and I felt lighter and more alive. But it was only later that I realized the gift he brought to us was the gift of delight. He is one of the few completely unwounded beings I have ever met and he greets everything he encounters with trust and delight. He evokes those same qualities in me and is a reminder that sacred space is at the heart of creation and lives in all our hearts as well. I call it Original Joy.

> 66 Joy is a reflection of our true nature —
> a pure, timeless, inviolable spirit found
> in each of us. 99 – Jack Kornfield

Journey Questions

When has God crossed your willful path?

What gifts did you receive?

Joan Garrabrant is a local therapist and writer. A former Chrysalis Board member, Joan continues to serve on the Advisory Council.

Memory Making

by Jason Hill

This is one of the great secrets and a key to being more present. All of us have memories, yet how many of you choose to make memories? Those who make that choice are engaging life in each moment. Go out and make a memory!

On occasion we have the good fortune to hear a piece of advice or a perspective that resonates. I recall feeling shifted into such a new perspective when I was at a concert and, between sets, the performer challenged us with the opening quote. Her wish was for each and every one of us in attendance to step out of that performance space and step into the world — onto our respective stages — more fully engaged in our lives.

This more fully engaged manner is how I have chosen to live in recent years. Traveling internationally, embarking on new career endeavors, attending workshops, experiencing relationships and facing health challenges are among the scenes and acts in this unfolding drama. In my reality, I am mentally shapeshifting and embracing a new approach, shifting my perceptions to bring into view something more.

Before the most recent Chrysalis Board meeting commenced, I overheard a rich exchange between two of the members. One was sharing the Native

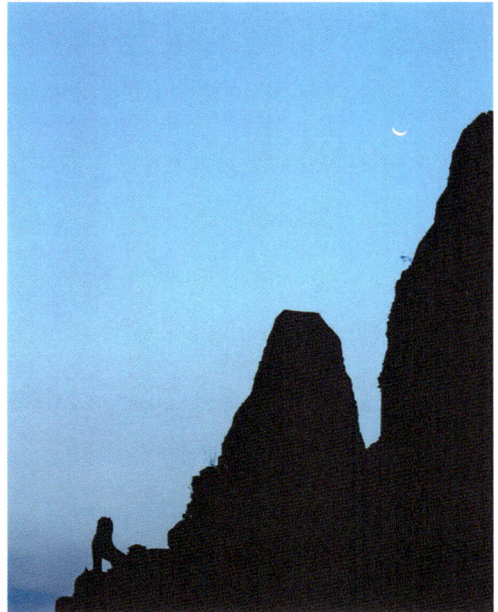

Jason Hill

66 It is not enough to find your passion . . . you must dive straight into the fire of your fear — where you can grab it and hold it until it transforms you. 99
– Bone Sigh Arts poster

American perspective of the medicine wheel and its correlation to living cyclically and in balance with the natural world. She commented that the season of fall is in the position of the West on the wheel. Leo Rutherford, in *Teachings of the Medicine Wheel — Ancient Wisdom for Modern Times,* writes, "The West is the place of Grandmother Earth who gives life and who teaches of cycles and patience, of the permanence of change, of death, decay and rebirth, and that Death-Gives-Life and all things are born, live, die, decay and give new life."

New life — something more along the lines of making memories that do not center around external factors, but instead encompass and liberate that which lies within. My "fully engaged" approach brings consciousness to the edge of great mystery, where my connection to the known dives into the depths of spirit. Internally, I foster a connection to something more that may lead to blinding Truth, yet with unwavering certainty some of my life's richest memories will be made.

What is the next memory you will choose to make?

A place of introspection encouraged me — as if a little voice was prompting, *Why not? Carpe diem!* — to go with friends to a weekend class. During the course of that weekend, I chose to attend and was mesmerized by the African drummer who offered a concert one evening. The ripple effect of her gifts — music and words — has prompted me to look deeper and with a keener eye as I live the power of making memories — and sharing them. The collective power yielded by seemingly simple and inconsequential choices (for those who have memories) reminds me to choose — again and again — following my inner guidance. Making each day richer with memories I'll cherish.

Beauty is in the eye of the beholder . . . and the life of the maker of memories.

> 66 The real voyage of discovery consists not in exploring new landscapes, but in having new eyes. 99 – Marcel Proust

Journey Suggestions

Give yourself permission, instead of attending to all of your external projects, to focus some attention on an intangible, inner-work session.

 The next time you are at the bookstore or library, instead of going to your favorite section, go to the section that least appeals to you. Take a book from the shelf, flip to a section and read a few pages. This is one of the ways to figure out something you may not know.

Jason Hill is always looking for meaningful connections and understanding. A former Chrysalis board member, he continues to serve on the Chrysalis Council of Advisors.

Anam Cara

by Susan Brock Wilkes

Bridget of Kildare is my kind of saint. Famous in Celtic spirituality, she is known for having twice performed the miracle of turning water to beer!

While this capacity is certainly an appealing quality, I am also drawn to Bridget's strong encouragement of spiritual friendship. It is said that when her foster son came to visit her, she intuitively sensed that his soul friend had died. She counseled him to seek a new one right away, noting that "anyone without a soul friend is like a body without a head." People then believed that the soul resided in the head and so she was using an image that they would immediately understand. The suggestion was that we are incomplete without spiritual friendship, that it is critical for the life of the soul.

66 This solitary work cannot be done alone. 99 – Ira Progoff

The rising popularity of Celtic Christianity has made us more aware of elements in this stream of the tradition such as the Celts' strong sense of God's immanence in the natural world, their awareness of the sacred in everyday life, respect for the leadership and gifts of women, and the fluidity of constructs of time and space. "Anam" is the Gaelic word for soul and "cara" for friend. Thus, Anam Cara is the soul friend, a concept which is uniquely valued in Celtic spirituality. Originally, the Anam Cara was a teacher, spiritual guide, or confessor to whom one could reveal the inner workings of one's heart and mind. Author Edward Sellner, in his book titled *The Celtic Soul Friend*, notes that the role evolved beyond this more formal one to a broader practice associated with healing, ongoing transformation and spiritual mentorship. The Anam Cara was a personal, intimate relationship of affection and depth, characterized by mutuality and shared wisdom. The friendship was one rooted in the spirit, thus making the participants "friends of God."

The Anam Cara relationship was not only something Bridget advised for others, but also expressed in her own life. Numerous poems and blessings in the Celtic collection *Carmina Gadelica* speak of the ways in which Bridget's soulful companionship, even after she was no longer physically present on earth, graced the authors' lives. Indeed, quite a few of the Celtic saints are said to have traveled great distances to spend time with those they regarded as soul friends.

This ancient practice and recognized social construct of Celtic life has much to offer us in the pace and complexity of our times today. It may well be that spiritual friendship is even more critical for the life of the contemporary soul than it was in Bridget's time. As Ira Progoff notes, our journeys are full of "solitary work." The Celts also valued solitude and contemplation as important for the spiritual path. Indeed, the ideal Celtic recipe for soulmaking balances extensive private meditation time with intensive spiritual relationships.

In its simplest form, the companionship and encouragement of a soul friend can enhance our sense of belonging to the world and aid us in overcoming isolation. As beautiful as that alone is, soul friendship is more than this; true spiritual metamorphosis happens in community. In *Anam Cara,* his book on Celtic wisdom, John O'Donohue explains how, in the context of the Anam Cara relationship, our inner landscape may be explored and illuminated in ways which are not possible alone. He notes that the deep affection found in such a friendship alters perception, bringing integration and healing. As he explains, "when your affection is kindled, the world of your intellect takes on a new tenderness and compassion."

In addition to enhancing integration of intellect and heart-knowing, the Anam Cara provides a rich source of insight into the symbolic aspects of life, synchronicities and dreams. There is a wonderful story in the Celtic tradition where

> " Friendship, then, is not to be reduced to an exclusive or sentimental relationship; it is a far more extensive and intensive force. "
> – John O'Donohue

Ciaran went to commune with his spiritual mentor, Enda. Both see the same vision of a tree growing beside a stream in the middle of Ireland, protecting the island and spreading its fruit. Enda offers an interpretation of the vision, noting "The great tree which you saw is you, Ciaran." They then explore what this may mean for his life; he later founds a spiritual community on the banks of a stream in the center of Ireland.

The Anam Cara is a relationship which acts as a chrysalis in which the truths of our lives can be revealed, the workings of the soul explored, discernment and insight offered, and wisdom shared. Through having and being an Anam Cara, we may indeed find that a sacred space has been created, a place where we may be held, "gentle and firm," as mystery plays out.

> But we do know how essential
> The chrysalis is,
> This place that holds
> Gentle and firm
> For the mystery to play out
> As we get our wings.
>
> – Joan Garrabrant

Journey Suggestions

Reflect on a soul friend who has enriched your spiritual life and the gifts she or he has brought you. Consider a way of expressing your gratitude for this transforming presence in your life.

Are there potential soul friends of whom you have not been fully aware or with whom you have not been fully present? Contemplate how you might bring one of those relationships to fruition such that it becomes a more "extensive and intensive force" in your life.

Reflect on the spiritual friendship you provide to others. What qualities might you offer to others on their spiritual journey?

Susan Brock Wilkes, Ph.D., is a spiritual director, leadership coach, and facilitator. A former president of Chrysalis, she continues to serve on the Council of Advisors and to lead programs for Chrysalis.

Spiritual Practices

Resonance

by Kay Davidson

MW Nea

> **When something is of us, is for us, it sets off a tuning fork inside us. It resounds because it has always been there. The resonance within us cannot be willed; it happens.** – James Hollis

A few years ago, I was asked by a Buddhist teacher about what had sparked my interest in Buddhism. She told me that many came to Buddhism through the path of suffering. Was this true of me as well? I replied that no, it was not. I had been fortunate in that no tragic life experiences had motivated my exploration. Rather, I answered, upon my first exposure to the Buddhist world view and the principles of its practice I had felt a "resonance" at a deep level of my being. The ideas seemed to fit me; they "rang true" for me in a way that certain Christian beliefs never had. And, as I was to learn, Buddhism is all about the experiencing of its beliefs through practice so that an individual can then discern for herself what is true.

Leaving thought systems aside, though, it seems to me that resonance has a broadly instructive — *even transcendent* — role to play in clarifying our lives. Resonance, as Hollis writes, is about what calls to us — to each of us individually. It is about locating ourselves in the universe — in that infinite realm of possibilities — by recognizing that which strikes the "tuning fork" within our unique snowflake of being. It is not agreement; that's cognitive. It is not consent; that is somehow social. It is, rather, an "Ah . . . this" and it is a bodily "YES!"

Edward Hirsch describes this experience through his relationship with poetry as being "when you feel encountered and changed by a poem, when you feel its seismic vibrations, the sounding of your depths." Reading the first chapter of his wonderful book, *How to Read a Poem*, is a little like spying on a passionate affair between a lover and his beloved. The chapter sings of resonance. What Hirsch describes there is a profoundly intimate relationship between a person and the source of his resonance. It's a relationship that can continually seduce one further and further into its sphere until knowing the source more fully is the same as the unfolding of one's own deepest nature. Or, if those "seismic vibrations" are ignored, it's a relationship that can become a pesky irritant, persisting in calling itself to one's attention; ultimately, if dismissed for too long, it can lead to the soul's regret — buried as a piece of what Jung would call the "unlived life."

There is something of ourselves to be learned in every experience of resonance. Discovering the nature of that something helps put us in tune with the universe, in harmony with its heartbeat. The reciprocal of the relationship with resonance is in the revelation of what is ours to name and to bring to light, what

> " The encounter with the numinous is available to those who have learned to listen for the resonance, who have surrendered the appeal of comfort to the summons of depth. "
> – James Hollis, *The Archetypal Imagination*

in the world each of us can make known in a way that no other snowflake can make known. It invites us, then obliges us to participate in the unfolding not only of ourselves, but in the unfolding of the universe.

"Resonance," says Hollis, "is the surest guide to finding our right path. It constitutes an inner guide amid the imposing images of the outer world and the constant traffic of the intrapsychic world . . . To hear it, one must be attentive, faithful, courageous enough to break from the power of the other cacophonous sounds and hear the resounding of our soul's intent."

Journey Questions

Have you experienced resonance? What was it like? How did you know it? Has it been instructive? In what way?

Have you ignored a resonance? Has it hounded you or become a regret? Is it really too late?

Kay Davidson teaches meditation and mindfulness and is a certified spiritual mentor.

The Art of Not Knowing

by Peggy C. Siegel

After telling a close friend that I finally understood a dream from eight years ago, she remarked, "Peggy, you are so good at not knowing!"

I laughed. "Is that a compliment?" Is it actually worth acknowledgment to be good at *not* knowing? We spend so much of life showing teachers, bosses and others what we *know*. Our value and competence and often our earnings are determined by what we can show that we know. My work in the world teaching courses, public speaking, writing and even my healing practice has been about sharing what I know.

So now that I am well into my fifties, I'm good at *not knowing*? Actually though, this is a compliment I take to heart. For years now I have deliberately and consciously practiced something I call the "Art of Not Knowing."

MW Nea

> 66 We cannot learn, that which we think we already know. 99 – Anonymous

Originally, I called it the "State of Not Knowing," but this implied a static or stationary place that I might find myself stuck in. It made me fear that I would *never* know. Then I began calling it the "Art" because one of Webster's definitions of art is "the creative and nonscientific branches of knowledge." Creative, nonlinear, intuitive forms of knowing are what I have access to if I am willing to stay and ride the experience of not knowing.

The practice of the Art of Not Knowing works like this. I become conscious of something I would like to know but don't know. For example, I spent two years writing full-time. Some of it was memoir writing, some essays, and some conceptual writing in the form of charts and outlines. In this case, I didn't know whether to share my writing, and if I did, what form I should put it in. Other examples of not knowing might include relationships (should I continue in this relationship?), work (am I to change jobs?), what a dream means, or what I am to know from a particular life experience.

First, I practice recognizing that I don't know the answer to these wonderings. I stop striving to know. I remember that time and space are needed for the not knowing. I find that I need time to go inside myself to see what is up. I need time for stillness and quiet. I remind myself that I have no control over when or how I will know. When I stay with the not knowing, the outcome is almost always a surprise. I practice patience . . . waiting. I notice dreams, synchronicities, body messages, and intuition. I allow myself to be open to knowing. Then I wait some more.

So . . .

I stop striving to know the answer.

I practice patience.

I notice.

In the meantime, I continue living my life. I still have responsibilities to family, friends, and work that need to be considered. This means I must find ways to take breaks from these responsibilities in order to give myself space to be in not knowing. Herein lies the challenge — *to live* with not knowing.

Although I find not knowing very frustrating (I mean I'd much rather know!), I also have noticed that it serves a purpose. If I can hold the tension and stay with it, at some point I will know more. Opening to not knowing is done with a trust that something is there for me in the not knowing. There will be guidance. There will be clarity. It is faith that if I stay in this place that eventually I will get it. In order to do this I must give up control over the timing, what I will get and how it will come to me. And I must trust that when I finally come to a place of knowing, I will recognize it internally.

So I continue the practice with trust.

I am often then rewarded. My body may suddenly feel at ease or I'll feel very clear. I may have an "aha" moment when I just suddenly know. But certainly the greatest benefit of staying with not knowing long enough is that when I come to this place of knowing, I am certain that what I have come to know is the truth. I know it in my whole being. And *that* is so worth the wait.

> " The Art of Not Knowing includes the practices of quiet mind, patience, stillness, allowing, and trust. "
> – Peggy Siegel

Journey Questions

Where are you experiencing uncertainty, or not knowing, in your life right now?

How could you practice patience?

Everyone's "aha" moments are different. In the past, how have you recognized when you finally reached a place of clear knowing?

Peggy C. Siegel, M.S., an intuitive energy healer in private practice, has taught numerous classes on intuition, energy work and personal spirituality. She has also published two books on sexuality and most recently completed a spiritual memoir, titled, *Teaching Albert Einstein to Fly*. A former president of Chrysalis, she continues to serve on the Chrysalis Council of Advisors.

Labyrinth Walk

by Elizabeth Keller Whitehurst

MW Nea

66 No one serves us but ourselves. No
one can and no one may. We ourselves
must walk the path. 99 – Buddha

The Winter Solstice at the Chrysalis Outdoor Labyrinth — and I have no business being here. The holidays! As usual, I still have much left to do. But wearing a light jacket on this unseasonably warm, December 21st late afternoon, I feel I'm where I really belong. I glance up as dark, steel-wool clouds gather, filling the air with expectation, like a summer storm's brewing.

Already the labyrinth's paths have been outlined with candles — round the center, outer ring and turning points. Joining a small group, we line up to begin our journeys one at a time. We observe silence, each with candle in hand, staving off the quiet darkness quickly falling on this shortest day of the year. A young neighborhood boy watches from the side, hands on hips, curious. My turn comes. In I go.

And so, I walk. Slowly. Mindfully. Calming. Centering. Letting my breath fall in with my slow and steady pace. I smile, nod to friends, people I know. And to strangers. We walk on. Nothing to say — nothing to be said.

Except for a voice inside me. *You are on your own path.* The message fills me both with a sense of soaring freedom and with deep longing.

I continue on my path. At times, I'm sure I'll run right into one of my fellow pilgrims, as we follow the curves together. Or it seems I'll need to stop for someone ahead of me or someone behind, whom I will pass or let her pass. No. It doesn't happen. I'm on my own path — and so are they.

Through this labyrinth dance, as we weave in and out, in patterns that the labyrinth sets, not us, I see as never before — *I am* on my own path. Though I enjoy the company of all those walking with me. The same people turn at the same time I do, walk beside, before or behind me. After a while, I reach points where I'm certain I'm coming out of the labyrinth. But then my path turns, leads me back in. Even when I start to feel tired, my centeredness wandering back to "to-do"s. Again and again, sure it must be the end of the journey, the path tricks me — back in I go.

More and more people join us, lining up, their candles illuminating their faces in the dying light, waiting their turns to enter the labyrinth. I think of all those walking now, of friends I know will walk later this evening, of all who have walked before and all who will walk in the future. Of all these many beings. We may walk alongside each other. Keep each other company. Smile and encourage our companions. Nod. Walk together for a time. Then we must go our separate ways, follow our own journey, our own path. All those I seek to help, all who break my heart with their sorrow, whom I yearn to save . . . no, I am on my own path — and so are they. Those who don't understand me, for not walking their path . . . no, I cannot walk theirs — they cannot walk mine. I am on my own path.

> 66 Pursue some path, however narrow
> and crooked, in which you can walk
> with love and reverence. 99
> – Henry David Thoreau

Even those we love most dearly, who've walked with us most of our lives, still walk a separate path of their own—as do we. Each life's path unique — a path of adventure, longing, freedom, sorrow, joy. Each soul called on a journey soley her own. Until at last, we rest from all the twists and turns, the false endings that send us back into the labyrinth, to begin again — when finally our journeys are through.

Tonight, we share light with our companions in the darkness of our walk. The candles others spread along the labyrinth path itself still light our way. The wind picks up. Rain's coming. My candle flame bobs and flickers but doesn't go out. Even here, on the darkest day of the year, there is light.

Journey Suggestions

Take time to walk the Chrysalis Outdoor Labyrinth (3318 Loxley Road, on the campus of Union Theological Seminary, Richmond, Virginia), or another labyrinth, yourself. Reflect on: How is your path unique?

How has it remained the same from the beginning of your life? How has it changed?

Give thanks for those who have accompanied you and been a witness to your journey.

Elizabeth Keller Whitehurst has spent many years writing and teaching. Liz has served on the Chrysalis Board.

The Practice of Blessing

by Susan Brock Wilkes

Adrian Luxmoore

66 The quiet eternal that dwells in our souls is silent and subtle; in the activity of blessing it emerges to embrace and nurture us. 99

– John O'Donohue

I've been listening to Barbara Brown Taylor's book, *An Altar in the World*, on audiotape. It's a beautiful book about being alive in our messy world and about practices that help us see the holy all around us. In the chapter titled "The Practice of Blessing," blessing is used as a verb. It means to sanctify or consecrate, to pronounce holy. Taylor notes how many of us tend to demur from blessing because we don't see ourselves as the appropriate one to pronounce something holy. Or, it doesn't even occur to us to bless everyday events and objects of our lives because we don't see them as sacred. She believes when we bless everyday events and things, we aren't so much conferring holiness as noticing the holiness that is already there.

One line in particular has stuck with me. Speaking of this practice of blessing, Taylor insistently says, "I'm telling you — the world needs you to do this." Now, Barbara Brown Taylor is an award-winning preacher so she is pretty darn convincing when her strong voice comes resounding out of your car speakers. She sounded like an old friend telling me what she really thought — "Susan, the world needs YOU to do this!"

Her directive reminds me of the ancient Celtic practice of blessing. The early Celtic Christians never saw a separation between spirit and matter, between this world and the sacred. The *Carmina Gadelica* is a collection of Celtic hymns and prayers that sings of the sacredness in everyday life. There are blessings for the smooring of the fire at night, praise hymns for the rising of the sun each morning and even a prayer to be said while driving cows.

In a class I once took, we were asked to adopt this practice and write blessings for everyday activities. What started out as a light-hearted attempt to appease my teachers by blessing my morning coffee changed as I wrote. A sense of reverence came over me as I became more aware of the miracle of the seedlings growing into full coffee plants, the richness of the soil from which they came, and the beauty of the laborer's hands that had picked the beans thousands of miles away. I prayed that the coffee might awaken in me a new sense of the Divine Presence in all things and a greater awareness of my connection with lives far away. Not only does the world need me to bless it, but I need the transformation that comes when I see its holiness.

I've since used the blessing writing activity with others. "Bless my minivan," one woman wrote. Seeing her carpool duties with fresh eyes, she prayed that her minivan might be a sanctuary for the teenagers she drove each day, a place where they might find peace in the midst of stormy adolescence. I smiled as one woman began reading a blessing for her turtle. She asked for peace to be laid "like the palm of a loving hand over his shell." She — and we — saw anew the hand of the Creator in even this small creature.

Getting in the habit of pronouncing holiness enables us to look more deeply within the ordinary events of our lives and see the sacred right here. The practice of blessing people, of seeing each other's holiness, can be even more powerful. The author Rachel Naomi Remen describes a beautiful ritual of blessing that her grandfather bestowed on her each week when she was little. It was the time she felt closest to God and she worried when he died whether God would even see

66 How many of us were taught actually to look for God within creation and to recognize the world as the place of revelation and the whole of life as sacramental? 99 – J. Philip Newell

her anymore. But, she realized later how her grandfather's early gift graced her whole life. You see, she came to see herself through his eyes and to understand that "once blessed, always blessed." Years later when her mother was very old, Rachel told her about her grandfather's practice of blessing and the impact it had had on her. Her mother smiled at her sadly and said, "I have blessed you every day of your life, Rachel. I just never had the wisdom to do it out loud."

This practice of noticing the holy around us and pronouncing it blessed is transformative. And we each have this spiritual capacity within us. May we bless every day of our lives and may we have the wisdom to do it out loud.

Journey Suggestions

Think about an everyday activity or object such as drinking coffee, a minivan, or a pet. Write a blessing for it and reflect on the sacredness present in the ordinary events of your lives.

Write a blessing for a person you care about. Consider whether you might share it with him or her.

Susan Brock Wilkes, Ph.D., is a spiritual director, leadership coach, and facilitator. A former president of Chrysalis, she continues to serve on the Chrysalis Council of Advisors and to lead programs for Chrysalis.

Creativity

Fabricating to Tell the Truth: My New Hampshire Summer

by Lenore H. Gay

A thousand souls in this southern city sit by their windows in the evenings. They watch the sun fade and the street lights wink on. While walking home on the street below I glance up at my own building, running my eyes over its surface but never see another face looking back.

My building looks lonelier than most. When dusk enfolds maples and wide sidewalks and the shadows obscure the buildings, I turn from the window to my walls lined with books filled with reedy old voices encased in covers. Men and women who have never talked in this life sit side by side on shelves, until someone new comes along and separates them. I imagine book covers disappearing, pages facing each other, voices from various centuries.

My room in graduate school was cluttered with books on poetry, pedagogy, fiction and papers. The day after graduation, I packed boxes for hours. I was 26 at the beginning of a summer that unfolded by accident. Driving home through New Hampshire, I stopped at a roadside diner for lunch. While at a picnic table by the highway eating a hot dog with relish and drinking a coke, the light streamed through the white poplars lining the road. A cool breeze suddenly flipped the leaves into shimmer white. Unlike the feverish stale air of the south, the clear air glowed. By the time I finished my hot dog, I was smitten, wondering why not stay, there's no reason to rush home, no one is waiting for me. I have a bit of money saved. Stay for the summer and begin work on the novel.

From my rented one room cottage on the Isle of Shoals I followed a rough trail down to the cliffs, assuming the rocks would be gray and brown. I was surprised to find they were mottled pink and green and blue. Each day around noon I visited the cliffs with a jug of water. I examined the encrusted rocks, ran my hands over their sharp, bumpy surfaces that didn't change day to day. Yet if enough has happened in your life, 26 is old enough to understand even color fades if you sit with it long enough.

MW Nea

The summer days took on a pattern, writing all morning, lunch and walking, and writing again in late afternoon until about eight when I'd walk into town for a seafood dinner. The most splendid day came at summer's end. Instead of writing I spent the morning on the rocks, with the sun overhead. I shed my clothes and felt the wind everywhere, it pummeled me and the cliff, shredded the clouds and diffused the heat of the sun. Waves slammed the rocks, birds screeched by. The beach below, narrow at noon turned into wide sand and shallows by four.

Could I make a living on the Isle of Shoals? Sadly, no.

Now in the evenings at my city window, I recall that summer. I don't think much about what has happened since I left New Hampshire twenty years ago, my good publishing job in a southern city far from the ocean and clear air.

But those cliffs and ocean stayed with me. Those vivid rocks and roiling ocean appear in thirty-six photographs and five sketches I made, using pastels on rough watercolor paper to get the light and shade and texture right. These scraps of paper stay in a manila envelope in my writing desk, I look at them, each month or so. But how many days did it rain in New Hampshire that summer? Did my landlord really ask me to go to the movies? He had a reddish beard, wore a white porkpie hat with the brim turned down and sailed in his free time. I can't remember the name of the movie we saw or even his name. I'm no longer confident that summer unfolded in the exact way I recall it now. Not at all.

Did that summer start the process by which I'll keep measuring significant things? Yes, the summer of my twenty-sixth year marked me in ways I'm still discovering.

*　*　*

I wrote the above fragment in May 2001 and abandoned it. Recently I revised it to use for a reading because it was short enough to read in under five minutes. I told the audience that someday I'd finish the piece because I thought it wanted to become a short story. After the reading a man asked how I liked my summer in New Hampshire. How did its climate compare with Richmond's heat? Did I finish writing my novel? Did I date my landlord all summer?

I said no, I was never in New Hampshire, I made it up. My inspiration came from a painting of the shoals in New Hampshire. No, I never made sketches of any place. I didn't date my landlord, didn't study English in graduate school or work in the publishing business.

> 66 Passion for the truth is an idea with more than one face. It includes the determination to look closely and long, to be unsatisfied with the secondhand and assumption. It also hints that only the hunger for something beyond the personal will allow the writer to break free of one major obstacle to originality — the fear of self-revelation. 99
> – Jane Hirshfield, *Nine Gates*

The Oxford English Dictionary defines a lie as an intentionally false statement, while to fabricate is defined as a construction, invention or concoction. Telling an intentional falsehood is beside the point in fiction writing, rather, fiction should not be constrained by facts. Part of the fun of fiction writing is interlacing research and experience with images and inspiration that might plummet like a bird from bright air or rise up from the morass of the unconscious. I've discovered even when I fabricate, the emotional truth worms its way into the narrative.

To write fiction is to be continually surprised.

> 66 Originality requires an aptitude for exile.
> Such independence may be of ideas,
> or it may be of style; in the end the two
> are the same. As is the result: a solitude
> that however difficult, is also held in
> affection — even if an affection sometimes
> mixed. 99 – Jane Hirshfield, *Nine Gates*

Journey Suggestions

Experiment, start with an image, a recurring thought, a sentence you read that sticks with you. Describe the image, wonder what might happen next and after that. Don't worry about whether it "really" happened. Write beyond the cliche description. Dig deeper. Don't destroy early drafts. Re-read what you wrote. How is it true? Keep writing and the worms will emerge.

Lenore H. Gay writes most days . . . fiction and poetry.

Intuitive Painting: Process Not Product

by Priscilla Burbank

Priscilla Burbank

> 66 Everyone is good at what comes to them spontaneously. 99
>
> – Michele Cassou

Most children believe they are artists. Ask any five-year-old! Most adults believe they are not creative and have no artistic talent. Maybe someone scolded us for coloring outside the lines, told us that trees aren't pink or gave us a "C" in art class. Drawing and painting became efforts to produce a product approved by external judges (parents, teachers, art critics) and only a few talented individuals were capable of creating this kind of art. We came to believe that we had no talent and we stopped painting. We stopped having fun.

This happened to my young neighbor, Carolyn, who often dropped by to "color" with me. Armed with oil pastels, we happily amused ourselves at the kitchen table. Sometimes, cookies were involved. A few years later, Carolyn declared that the picture she'd drawn of her dog didn't look like him and started to tear it up. I told her she'd captured her dog's spirit while running with his ears flopping up and down. Her pictures didn't have to look like photographs — they could show the feelings of things. Carolyn tried drawing "feelings of things" and laughed at her crazy pictures.

Since I had been painting intuitively for a few years at this point, I knew how the critical words we tell ourselves stop the creative process in its tracks. Intuitive painting requires you to recognize and let go of the "inner critic" in order to access your innate creativity — the creativity you possessed when you were a little child. This is not easy, but it is worth the effort.

Michele Cassou, the originator of intuitive painting, quit studying art — frustrated by the criticism and competition. She saw young children painting with abandon at a Paris studio and asked to join them, experiencing the freedom of painting without goal or purpose. She spent the next 30 years developing techniques to help people unlearn the critical self-talk that blocks the creative process. To Cassou, art is simply "deep and essential play."

I experienced how powerful the inner critic can be when I took a Batik class in Bali, thinking it would be relaxing. I had done nothing artistic since seventh grade, but after years of practicing corporate law and raising two children, I was ready for some creativity. Our teacher, Nyoman, told us to draw a picture on canvas. I panicked. *What? I can't draw.* Having paid for the class, I somehow managed to draw a tropical scene. Next, we had to outline our drawing with hot wax. My hands shook. I was going to ruin it. Soon I was sweating and getting short of breath.

Nyoman said, "Chill out baby. You can't do art and think. Meditate . . . no thinking!" I couldn't stop the chatter in my head. I started to pay attention to it. *Where's the panic coming from? It won't be good enough?* After some difficult internal dialogue, I told myself that I wouldn't be shot if the Batik turned out poorly. *Whoa, where was that coming from?* I calmed down. *Just breathe!*

Then, the fun started. Painting inside the wax lines! I love bright colors and found that I was having fun. I wasn't criticizing myself. I was in the moment. I could breathe away my inner critic, whose voice spoke frequently, and engage in the creative process.

I soon had an opportunity to take an intuitive painting workshop. After Bali, it sounded intriguing. Our facilitator asked that we not comment on each other's works, even to praise them, as positive judgments can inhibit the creative process as much as negative ones. Pamela asked us to pick up our brushes, dip into the first color that caught our eyes and fill the page with color. "Make it juicy!" I found myself choosing one of my least favorite colors — orange. "Turn the paper around, use your non-dominant hand and keep painting." Except for the orange, this was fun!

Then, Pamela asked us to dialogue with our painting — which sounded ridiculous. "Write blah, blah, blah, until something comes up." Starting with "blah, blahs," I wrote, "What was up with the orange?" It got profound pretty quickly as it created insight into my relationship with my mother. By the end of the workshop, I was hooked.

Pamela suggested buying inexpensive paper and oil pastels and recommended Cassou's book, *Life, Paint and Passion*. I started scribbling and journaling, then found someone to work with who had trained with Cassou! Many workshops, retreats and a year-long certification process later, my intuitive painting continues to amaze me. The colors, images and rhythms I feel while painting have opened me to a host of emotions and have led to many significant insights. It is a profound spiritual practice. Dealing with the inner critic is a challenge, but when I am able to distance myself from it, I experience presence and connection to something I think of as the creative spirit, that seems to flow through me when I paint! It is harmony.

> " Every child is an artist. The problem is how to remain an artist when we grow up. "
> – Pablo Picasso

Journey Suggestions

Buy cheap paper and oil pastels or tempera paint and a few brushes.

Pretend you are five.

Paint what you would paint if it didn't matter.

Trust the brush.

Have fun!

Priscilla Burbank is the current president of The Chrysalis Institute. A retired attorney inspired by a Chrysalis program on Consciousness, Priscilla discovered intuitive painting while pursuing a master's degree in The Evolution of Consciousness from The Graduate Institute in Connecticut.

A Poetic of Change

by Beith Burton

B Milner

66 You must revise your life. 99

– William Stafford

This semester, I'm attending my first college literature class in 25 years. Many of my younger classmates, attending college for the first time, are not quite sure what to expect from me. I can see the questions in their eyes when we work together —

Why aren't you at home, raising a family, like my mother does?

And then the statement:

I hope, by the time I'm your age, I'll be finished with school.

I have a paper due soon, and I remember those days when my first draft was my only draft — those days when I thought I'd gotten away with something by writing my paper in 12 hours. These days, however, I'm far more interested in my second draft than my first. I think that's my answer to my classmates' questions: I'm here because I understand the value of revision.

In my poetry class, we talk about the enjambed line. While it might sound like sticking your thumb in a dike, it actually comes from an Old French term meaning "to straddle." An enjambed line is one in which the thought continues from one line to the next. The meaning "straddles" the lines.

Take, for example, a familiar college sentence:

I am thinking about changing my major from history to literature.

A couplet might look like this:

I am thinking about changing my major
from history to literature.

The first line of this couplet is an enjambed line. The thought straddles the first line, offers no conclusive punctuation, and doesn't finish up until the end of the second line, where there's a period to end the thought. The first line of this couplet is enjambed; the second line is "endstopped." A period, a comma, a semicolon, a dash, a question mark — all those things will endstop a line.

When outside of the poetic community, enjambed lines create havoc — punctuarians note the need for closure, editors note what's missing and get out red pens, conversationalists note that someone's lost a train of thought.

Now, take a look at what happens when the number of enjambed lines is increased — when the meaning is allowed to "straddle" an even wider gap from the beginning to end of the sentence:

I am thinking about changing
my major from history
to literature.

Look again at that first line:

I am thinking about changing

Another thing about enjambment: in poetry, the line is everything. Each line is considered an end in itself, whether it is endstopped or not. Each line has its own life — history, meaning, truth, can all be said to exist in a single line.

I am thinking about changing

Notice how much power now exists in this one line. Who of us does not know what it means? Who of us has not experienced the tension that change brings? Now, it does not matter if the sentence is started by a college freshman or a career-changer —the line speaks to us all, causes us all to take notice; to wait for the next line —

my major from history

Some of us might sigh, because we realize who is speaking now — but perhaps not. "My major from history" also carries some weight, some grav-ity, because of those two words at the end of the line — *from history* — since we've already seen ourselves in the word *changing,* the words *from history* can also

    One door opens; another shuts behind.
    One sun sets and another sun, she rises.
    Love comes to you in old, familiar ways;
    love comes to you in shadows and disguises.
    – Richard Thompson

help us understand that this *history* is *our* history, too.

to literature.

Ah, finally, we've come to the endstop. Yes, now, perhaps, the meaning is smaller. Yet, perhaps not — maybe, for a few seconds, we've had a glimpse into the world of the beginner, the uncertain college student trying to figure out the future. Maybe we've lent our understanding of that tension of change to someone else, without even knowing who that person is.

In the book *After Empire: The Art and Ethos of Enduring Peace*, theologian Sharon Welch describes a community she has encountered which has done amazing work for social justice over generations:

While at Harvard, I attended the weekly worship services of Harambee, the African American student group at the divinity school . . . I encountered in this moral tradition a radically different ethos and ethic, one that began where white middle-class thought and action often stopped. This ethic began with the realization that we cannot imagine how we will win.

Sometimes, the greatest power we have can come from what we do with the unknown — what power, what promise exists beyond a line we have already written?

Poetry is a study of the line; the study of what is broken and what is whole. Poetry is the study of what has not yet ended and the mystery of *not knowing what comes next.*

Journey Suggestions

Take a paragraph from your journal, or write one now, using paragraph form. Don't worry about where to put the words — just get some thoughts out on paper. Then, start enjambing your lines. See what messages your own writing has for you. Start a new conversation with yourself based on what you've found.

Take someone else's paragraph — perhaps a politician's speech, or a paragraph from a favorite book, or perhaps a reading you don't agree with. See what happens to the meanings when the lines are enjambed. Are they saying something else instead?

Beith Burton is a lifelong fan of Chrysalis. Her degree in theology now qualifies her to spend time making art and working in a machine shop making things out of metal. She has expertise in navigating life's left turns.

At Our Core

by Joan Garrabrant

> 66 Whether the film is a veil of culture, of memory, of mental or religious training, of trauma or sophistication, the removal of that film is the goal of all therapy and education. 99
>
> – Mark Nepo, *At Our Core*

Mark Nepo, in *The Book of Awakening*, says that each of us is born with an unencumbered spot of grace which, in the normal course of things, gets tarnished or covered over. Occasionally the covering gets worn through and we and others get a glimpse of "that uncorruptible spot of grace at our core." It is then that "we have moments of enlightenment, moments of wholeness . . . moments of clear living when inner meets outer, moments of full integrity of being, moments of complete Oneness." Recently I was fortunate to be in the presence of that unencumbered spot of grace as I witnessed an exchange between two of my granddaughters described in the following poem.

Two Poems, One Heart

Kali
Full of eight year-old fire, she
burst upon us,
Kodi and me.
"Gaba, I have
a question," she loudly proclaimed.
Then, seeing tears
on her sister's
cheeks, she softly
said, "What's happening here is more
important than
my question," and
she turned to leave.

MW Nea

Kodi

Opening her arms, Kodi called
to her, "Come here,
Kal. It's ok.
Ask your question."
And as they sat, these two sisters,
each making room
for the other,
I too was held
in the sure and certain knowledge
that no matter
what, these two girls
would be all right.

Mark Nepo gave words to what I saw embodied for a moment by these two young girls. In that exchange between them, I was given a tangible experience of what is meant by "namaste," when "the divine in me bows to the divine in you."

66 Namaste means I honor the place in you where the entire Universe resides; I honor the place within you of love, of light, of truth, of peace; I honor the place within you where, when you are in that place in you, and I am in that place in me, there is only one of us. 99

– attributed to Mahatma Gandhi

Journey Questions

Can you recall a time when the covering was worn through and you caught a glimpse of "that uncorruptible spot of grace at our core"?

When you reflect on the film or veil that had covered that unencumbered spot of grace, was the covering one of culture, of memory, of mental or religious training, of trauma, of sophistication, or of some other kind of covering?

Joan Garrabrant, LCSW, is a former Chrysalis Board member who now serves on the advisory board. She is a psychotherapist in private practice, the Co-Founder of Group Dreamwork Training Institute, and a SoulCollage facilitator. Her daily blog can be found at www.aholdingplace.com.

Inner Work

House as Mirror of Self

by Kathleen McSweeney

MW Nea

> 66 Home is a place of security within an insecure
> world, a sacred place in a profane world . . . 99
> – Kimberly Dove

If your home could talk to you, what would it say?

I think my modest house would mention first the front garden, nestled in a small courtyard, and the back garden, opening onto a walking path. In the front, I read or meditate. In the back, I say hello to dog walkers and cyclists and compare notes with fellow gardeners. Each entrance is vital, serving my needs for solitude and togetherness. It seems obvious now, but it took several years for me to see I had been choosing privacy and quiet or community and sharing by walking out either the front or the back door. The awareness has enhanced my delight in where I live.

I think my home would be grateful for its coziness and comfortableness. It would surely offer some constructive criticism as well, urging me to rethink a belief in Picasso's notion that every room in a house should be a studio. I'd be asked to discriminate among many creative and professional interests and let go of whole categories and their accoutrements. Letting go of related books and materials could prompt me to release a long held illusion of having all the time in the world to master and complete a multitude of projects.

What do you imagine your home would request of you?

I'm intrigued by what author Akiko Busch in *Geography of Home* refers to as "personalization of space," ways in which individuals and families instill their homes with special objects that not only indicate style preferences but also evoke reverence, connectedness to heritage, even aspirations. May Sarton calls these objects "the dear familiar gods of home." A sister who longs to live in Paris but isn't ready to move far from friends and family transformed her New York condominium into a charming Paris apartment. A family steeped in Buddhist thought displays Eastern expressions and prints throughout their home. A couple surrounds themselves with colorful folk art gathered in their travels together.

What might a visitor viewing your home learn about your philosophy, personality, hopes and dreams?

Many times we choose objects without full awareness of their meaning to us; uniting these outer actions with our inner thoughts can be gratifying. For several years, my family's refrigerator displayed views of Maine mountains and seas, joyfully photographed on hikes and boating trips. Over time, I realized the photographs were signals that I wanted to experience Maine in more depth. Within a year, my family and I moved to midcoast Maine and I began a job in Freeport. My years there were filled with adventure, old and new friends, and important professional growth.

What do prominently placed objects in your home evoke in you?

We may begin imagining or actually making changes in our homes without realizing the significance. Years ago, I realized that whenever I'm undergoing a major transition, I begin moving my books on their shelves, discarding those I'm no longer interested in, placing at eye level the readings I want to focus on. Now when I find myself rearranging my books, I ask myself what is changing within. Lillian Hillman said: "People change and forget to tell each other." I've found, in addition, we change and forget to tell ourselves.

As you look around your home, what indications do you see that you've changed or are in transition?

When we share a home, we can also share our ideas of what *home* means. Clare Cooper Marcus in *House as a Mirror of Self* suggests couples individually write down or draw what home means to them. One partner may dream of open spaces and lots of light, while the other partner may envision home as a cave, a nest of warmth and inclusion. Working together, they can introduce elements of both in different spaces of the home. Parents of young children may feel overwhelmed by toys and games spread out and need to reclaim some space for grown-up living. Adolescents' insistence on privacy often represents their need to begin forming their own separate identities. Weaving together how our home will look and feel can yield a sense of unity among all who live there.

Home can vary in meaning to us as we assume new roles. Single-again friends describe how inner journeys prompted external changes. A friend whose husband had died two years earlier described her struggle for self-permission to decorate in her own singular taste. As we looked at a newly designed room, she noted her inner progress as well. "I will always love my husband," she said, "and he would want me to live in the present."

A home can provide protection, healing and refuge. When we are conscious of the dynamic between our home and our psyche, we can intentionally create environments that promote peace and nurturance. A friend once told me her favorite word is "dwell," meaning creating a space where she can truly be herself to relax, rest, and recharge. In that spirit, may your home be a dwelling place.

66 The life we want is not merely the one we have chosen and made. It is the one we must be choosing and making. 99 – Wendell Berry

Journey Questions

If your home could talk to you, what would it say? What do you imagine your home would request of you?

What might a visitor viewing your home learn about your philosophy, personality, hopes and dreams?

What do prominently placed objects in your home evoke in you? As you look around your home, what indications do you see that you've changed or are in transition?

Kathleen McSweeney is a leadership coach, photographer, and Chrysalis Council member. Kathleen is active in a writing group whose members offer each other inspiring feedback and a book club where she experiences the richness a collaboration of voices can bring to any novel.

Emergence

by Jason Hill

Jason Hill

Mr. Fuji pointed to a small tree and indicated that his recently re-opened shop was akin to that tree. "It is small now and needs to be nurtured, but has the potential to grow into a lasting part of this community." His intention was not to force its growth, but instead to be with the process as it emerged.

On December 26, 2004, Southeast Asia emerged into the forefront of the world's media outlets and connected the minds and hearts of countless human beings. For many — all around the world — transitions of monumental proportions began that day. On top of the despair I felt for those suffering, the trip I'd just finished planning to paradise underwent a drastic and dramatic shift.

I chose to proceed with the trip, but altered

> "Our consciousness rarely registers the beginning of a growth within us . . . there have been many circulations of the sap before we detect the smallest sign of the bud."
>
> – George Eliot (Mary Ann Evans)

my plans. Serendipitously, I met Mr. Fuji, somewhere off the beaten path on an island in Southeast Asia in May, 2005. We stood a few hundred yards from the Andaman Sea, where waves gently lapped onto the shoreline of Ko Phi Phi. Six months earlier, where we stood was under several feet of water engulfed by a churning sea, reeling from the force of an earthquake hundreds of miles away.

While in Thailand that spring, I found myself amidst devastation — toppled trees, shattered buildings, overturned vehicles, scattered debris — all evidence of ruin from a Western perspective. Yet, in my conversations with Thais, the mindset of a predominantly Buddhist culture became evident. Acknowledging that the tsunami happened, but removing the focus from the past and shifting it to the present moment was commonplace among those with whom I spoke. My mindset began to shift from the focus on their loss and subsequent needs — where it had been since I first heard the news about the tsunami — to an awareness of potential. Potential I was able to grasp when I opened my eyes to see, my heart to feel and my mind to perceive a different perspective.

From shifts in perspective we hold the potential and the power to emerge from existing patterns. To shift our actions from a human-doing to a human-being is not always easy — but isn't it always possible? A charity event I was part of a few years ago used a slogan, where the word "impossible" had an apostrophe introduced to it and became "I'm possible."

Possibility surrounded me in Thailand. Striking examples of life's potential to prevail showed undeniably in the flowers. Most of the resorts were destroyed, but some of the deeply rooted landscaping remained. Occasional instances of red and yellow and white were scattered along the beachfront and among the pieces of rubble. An article I read years earlier in a publication, a short time after the eruption of Mount St. Helens, came to mind. The article indicated that

> 66 Don't fight the waves. Dive under, bob up, or catch the curl and ride the wave. The ocean is stronger than you: You might as well be a matchstick in comparison. But if you yield to the waves, they carry you. Their power becomes you. 99
> – Elizabeth Cunningham

the re-establishment of an ecosystem could be evidenced by the re-emergence of wildflowers. Though these flowers were not wild, they embodied the same untamed spirit of life prevailing. A stark juxtaposition of what some perceived as devastation or ruin contrasted by a flower in bloom — the cyclic power of nature's emergence.

The underlying sense that I am emerging into someone new, someone transformed and someone beyond my former expectations tends to soften my growing pains — how do you feel?

Journey Questions

What can you acknowledge about your life that encourages you to emerge into new ways of being?

What is deeply rooted in your conscious mind about your life?

What might you acknowledge about your life that could be liberated to permit you to step out of your shadows and into your light?

Jason Hill is always looking for meaningful connections and understanding. A former Chrysalis board member, he continues to serve on the Chrysalis Council of Advisors.

Satisfaction

by Kay Davidson

MW Nea

> 66 These few words are enough. If not these words, this breath. If not this breath, this sitting here. This opening to the life we have refused again and again. Until now. Until now. 99 – David Whyte

Not too long ago, my mother and I were having lunch at a favorite restaurant. The meal each of us had chosen was simple: a salad (mine Asian, hers more eclectic), water for a beverage and one breadstick apiece. I mention the particulars because of their ordinariness — food that appears on menus most anywhere in this country.

As our meal was ending, I said to my mother, "That was very satisfying." And she said to me in return, "Yes, it was." I then sat for a moment with the physical sense of being satisfied and with the kind of blank but complete feeling state that was a part of the experience. I was satisfied. I wanted nothing else to eat or drink. I had had just enough — not too much, not too little. I had left nothing in my bowl, nor had my mom. We each had consumed everything that was brought to us — each shred of carrot, each lettuce leaf — nothing wasted.

I then asked Mom how often she was aware of that feeling or experience of being satisfied; how often did it happen for her? She thought for a moment and guessed one or more times a day — but that she didn't know for sure. And I began to think about that. How often do I experience that kind of simple satisfaction without recognizing it or noting it but merely taking it for granted? Even though it really is a pleasant state, perhaps we often bypass such satisfaction because it's an uncomplicated experience, one that requires nothing else and one that is quite plain rather than richly embellished. At the level of our everyday lives, satisfaction may be too banal a pleasantness to register often in our awareness. We are programmed for more exciting sensations, for louder pleasures.

Yet, Rachel Naomi Remen's account of her mother's last words to her alerts us to the potential power of noticing and bringing more awareness to these gentler traces of happiness. Remen's mother, at age 84, was about to undergo cardiac bypass surgery; she was given only a 40% chance of surviving the procedure.

Remen writes:

Pulling me close, [my mother] kissed me and whispered, "No matter what happens here, I want you to know that I am satisfied." Then she smiled her charming, rakish smile and they took her away.

As it happened, her mother did not survive the operation. Remen, reflecting on these last words, doubted that it was her mother's considerable accomplishments in life that had given her such ease and contentment in the face of near certain death. Rather, she says her mother had left her with an important question: How do I live so I, too, might find a deep satisfaction at the end?

Perhaps, then, satisfaction is both simple and deep. As at lunch with my mother, there are those ordinary moments of noticing *just rightness,* a fleeting harmony of things, a temporary sense of well-being.

And beyond that, there is this notion of *enoughness,* of knowing how much of a thing is just right — how much work, how much play, how much stuff; a way of living into the wisdom of discerning between need and greed, between ease and indulgence, between completion and compulsive striving. And what if such discerning wisdom results from accumulating moments of satisfaction, so that the more we notice our fleeting contentments, the more we learn about what brings our lives into a deeply satisfying harmony?

> ❝Happiness is a place between too much and too little.❞ – Finnish Proverb

Journey Questions

Are you aware of satisfying moments? How can you become more so?

What would be necessary ingredients for a satisfying life?

Kay Davidson teaches meditation and mindfulness and is a certified spiritual mentor.

I Have All the Time I Need

by Angier Brock

MW Nea

> " Look back on time with kindly
> eyes — he doubtless did his best "
>
> – Emily Dickinson

I once taught a summer class in which teachers from various grade levels and disciplines explored the uses of writing in their classrooms. As part of the project, participants planned and led hour-long sessions in which they introduced the rest of us to some aspect of their writing research.

When it was his turn, one of them — I'll call him Joe — began by asking us to sit for five minutes in silence with the mantra, "I have all time I need." Even the skeptics among us were willing to try. The room grew still as we each got as comfortable as one can get in an academic setting and began, in silence, to breathe gently in and out: *I have all the time I need. I have all the time I need.*

It was, quite frankly, wonderful.

And it made Joe's arrival the next day all the more ironic. He came in late and rushing, his discombobulation evident in the papers and books that went flying as he burst into the room, breaking the hush in which the rest of us were already engaged in our morning journal writing. When he realized how intrusive his entrance was, he screeched to a halt and said, rather sheepishly and by way of apology, "My mantra lied."

We all laughed, but some fifteen years later, whenever I get pinched for time, I remember that story. This week, with several deadlines converging, I have been pinched for time — which is why I have been thinking about it.

Time. The older I get, the more time becomes one of life's great mysteries. I do not fathom how sometimes it creeps and sometimes it flies by, or how sometimes it is totally attached to yesterday and other times it is completely attracted to tomorrow. Several current popular books emphasize the goodness, the importance, really, of living in the Now. I have read some of them. I think I understand what their authors are getting at — and agree.

But several years ago, toward the end of my father's life, memory loss trapped him in a mostly perpetual *now*. Rarely could he remember the immediate past — a visit from a friend, or something he had read the day before. Even more rarely could he remember the promise of a future event — a grandson's upcoming wedding, or the expectation of the birth of a great-grandchild. When he spoke of frustration about his memory, I told him that he was becoming very zen. I said that some people practiced for years to be able to live so purely in the present.

"I'd rather stay a Methodist," he said. I was grateful that he never lost his sense of humor. But watching him, I realized how much comfort and pleasure — as well as pain and fear — come from remembering the past and anticipating the future.

Time. When I was young, I thought it was linear, like all those dates marching on the charts around the top of the history classroom. And so it is. But time is also curvilinear. It has curvatures in it — what Madeleine L'Engle has called "wrinkles." And even when I feel its pinch, time has a certain miraculous elasticity about it that gives, somehow, and leaves me feeling a little awed.

I wonder: What if Joe's mantra did NOT lie? What if it is true — that I have all the time I need? I have all the time I need. How might I live more fully into that truth? What changes might I need to make to do so? How about you?

> 66 This time, like all times, is a very good one, if we but know what to do with it. 99
> – Ralph Waldo Emerson

Journey Questions

How might you live more fully into the truth, *I have all the time I need?*

What changes would you need to make to do so?

A former Chrysalis Board member, Angier lives, writes and gardens in Yorktown, Virginia.

Mindfulness

Here

by James M. Burke

Readers of *Words for the Journey* are well-versed in the importance of living in the present and many are outstanding practitioners of this difficult art. We are surrounded by history — our own and that of others. The ghosts of the past generate at an astonishing rate. After all, history, as the documentary filmmaker Ken Burns noted, "is everything before this second . . . this second . . . this second." Being here in the present seems to go against everything. It goes against what we are told in our lives: have a vision for where the organization is going, plan for retirement, think through all the possibilities. When we fly, we are focused on our arrival time, and often fail to experience what we are flying over at various moments. I still remember the joy of a pilot announcing the Northern Lights on a trip to England years ago. There, over the speaker, was the voice of the present.

As has often been noted, looking back often conjures up feelings of regret and loss and looking ahead to the coming days and years can breed both anticipation and anxiety. Looking back and looking forward both have in common possibility. There is the possibility of what could have been and there is the possibility of what could be.

Though we can gain some joy in reflecting on the past upon moments that gave us happiness, we can also find ourselves falling into the abyss of regret. In the HBO series, *In Treatment*, the psychologist-protagonist struggles over how to let go of his guilt about his inability to save his mother from suicide when he was a teen, and wonders whether his life's work may have emerged from a desire to get it right. His struggles highlight a key question: how do we live very much in the here and now, embrace our past as the ground out of which we emerge, and still hope for better days ahead?

Let me offer two stories to focus our reflection on this question. First, in the documentary *Still/Here*, the choreographer Bill T. Jones and the journalist Bill Moyers explore dance and mortality. Being HIV-positive and losing his long-term partner, Arnie Zane, to AIDS, Bill Jones wanted to explore the meaning of people (including himself) facing life-threatening illnesses and being here despite it all. Moyers asks Jones what it means for him to be here. Jones says poignantly that here is: *a place where I can stand and not be distracted by pain, not be in the future, in the past. I can be loving. I can be responsive. Here is the New York City subway, when I have to be there. I'm rushing from one appointment to another, and I am worried, thinking, "Am I failing? Did I get a bad review yesterday? What is going to happen?" But, suddenly at that moment, I realize . . . my flesh, I'm upright, I'm doing. I'm not in bed, hooked up to a ventilator. I'm not connected to an IV. I say, "Hey, look. You're here. You are on your two feet."*

Jones is both painfully and beautifully informed by the past and by the future, but highlights moments of gratitude that can emerge because of and despite both of these. His reflections in the interview underscore that sadness and hope can both lead to a better now.

Second, Charles Dickens offers a perspective on Past, Present, and Future that continues to be inspiring. At the last leg of

> ❝ I will live in the Past, the Present, and the Future. The Spirits of all Three shall strive within me. ❞
>
> – Charles Dickens

Ebenezer Scrooge's nocturnal encounters with the Spirits, he asks the ethereal ghost of Christmas Yet-to-Come if the images of sadness he has been shown are images that must come to be or ones that can be changed. He begs the Spirit, "Assure me that I may change these shadows you have shown me, by an altered life . . . I will honor Christmas in my heart, and try to keep it all year. I will live in the Past, the Present, and the Future. The Spirits of all Three shall strive within me. I will not shut out the lessons that they teach."

Perhaps the greatest honor that we can pay the Present is to heed the lessons of the Past and to see the emerging lessons of the Future. *A Christmas Carol* is ultimately about a conversion to the Present, but it could never happen without the constant presence of the Past and the Future as sources not of judgment, but of information that ultimately allow something akin to freedom of choice in the Present. In the end, as we all know, it is only here where I can make a difference — however small that difference may be. The river rushes forward and we with it, present moment after present moment.

> 66 God made the world round
> so we would never be able
> to see too far down the road. 99
> – Isak Dinesen

Journey Questions

When was the last time you felt *here*? Return to that space and inhabit it again.

What do you notice?

What TV shows, movies, books or other works of art describe or elicit the experience of *being here*? Try and become more aware of these opportunities to study the art of *being here*.

Jim is the director of the Performance Management Group at VCU and enjoys taking time away from management consulting to think about the more spiritual dimensions of life. A psychologist by training, he very much values learning about the journeys of others as they go through life.

Moments of Being

by Peggy C. Siegel

B Millner

> " If your mind isn't clouded with unnecessary things, this is the best season of your life. "
>
> – Wu-Men

Time and again I keep finding myself thinking I know what "being present" is all about, only to be surprised by my next new experience of presence. Over and over both the concept and the experience seem to be growing in size.

At first I thought being present was just noticing — I am sitting here writing. There is soft music playing. I smell the candle and hear the nearby traffic. — This was a good way to practice paying attention to my life and I enjoyed life more by noticing what was happening in the present moment. But sometimes I wondered what the big deal was about being present.

Last fall I went to a week-long Buddhist Meditation Retreat with Tara Brach. The days were filled with sitting and walking meditations, yoga, guided meditations and teachings. One late afternoon, as I was doing a walking meditation in the woods, I came to an open marshy meadow brimming with human-sized wild flowers, milkweed, grasses and brambles all going to seed in the breeze. A backdrop of gold-leafed trees reflected the late day sun. As I stood amidst all these plants and seeds, I began to feel my own life energy blend in. Keeping a quiet mind, I just stood there, alive. Then, spontaneously, I began feeling — in my whole body — gratitude for life. My mind came in and started naming what I was grateful for. But as I stopped the words, quieted my mind and was merely standing there, I felt in my body that there was literally just gratitude itself. I was *being* grateful.

Over the week of meditation, as I continued practicing quieting the mind and becoming more aware of all that was in each moment, I had several more experiences of what I began to call "spontaneous upwellings." Another occurred during a close encounter with a deer who was only ten feet away. The deer had taken me by surprise and my natural reaction was to think about what I would tell people or wondering how long she would stay. Instead, with inner silence, we locked eyes and held perfectly still for minutes. Then, starting in my feet and coming up my body, my heart opened and I experienced an upwelling in my whole body of joyfulness. Just joy. Moments of *being* joy.

These spontaneous upwellings I experienced during that week, which eventually included joy, peace, gratitude and compassion, were momentary. I found that I can notice sensations in my body, sounds and sights around me and be so quiet that I get that — and the *more* that is present. Each time I also discovered this — that when I am awake and fully present, these very qualities are ultimately universally available any time in the spaciousness of the moment. They are not states that I create or will myself to have. I am not even holding an intention to experience the state. Rather, with a practice of quieting the mind, coming to inner stillness and noticing the moment itself — all kinds of gifts can arrive in the spaciousness. The surprise has been to see what is universally available in the experience of present moment awareness. And I don't need to be on retreat to be surprised.

I had a lovely spontaneous upwelling in the shoe store Saturday morning. As my grown daughter walked around in this huge warehouse of a shoe store trying out sparkly high-heels for her upcoming wedding, I sat on a small bench, guarding our purses and her stack of other selections. Just then, a young family with two little girls came by and I complimented the little girls on their matching silver-glittered shoes with red butterflies.

> 66 If we are to grasp the reality of our life while we have it, we will need to wake up to our moments. Otherwise, whole days, even a whole life could slip past unnoticed. 99
>
> – Jon Kabat-Zinn, *Wherever You Go, There You Are*

Suddenly the baby, twenty-one months-old, who was in her father's arms, took one look at me and leaned over to me with pick-me-up arms. The parents were surprised and meant to move on but she wouldn't have it. She wanted me and I wanted her. I asked her parents if I could hold her and with their permission put my arms out and she leaped into my lap. We just silently smiled and gazed at one another happily. It was pure love and sweetness. Being present only to the moment and holding this gentle, content baby.

Together, just being love.

If gratitude can arise from acres of weeds, and love itself arise in a shoe store, I wonder what can arise in this moment . . . and in this moment . . . and in this moment.

Journey Questions

What are you experiencing in this moment?

What helps bring you into the present moment?

Recall a moment where you were fully immersed in the experience of the present. What was your felt state?

Peggy C. Siegel, M.S., an intuitive energy healer in private practice, has taught numerous classes on intuition, energy work and personal spirituality. She has published two books on sexuality and most recently completed a spiritual memoir, titled, *Teaching Albert Einstein to Fly*. A former president of Chrysalis, she continues to serve on the Chrysalis Council of Advisors.

A Language of Nourishment

by Kathleen McSweeney

Kathleen McSweeney

Years ago when I entered the corporate world, one of my biggest surprises was the complex jerry-rigging often created when a manager was not willing to provide honest feedback to an underperforming employee. Managers would cite reasons such as fear of hurting the other individual or damaging an old friendship. To manage around the employee, colleagues would be assigned ad-

> 66 At some time, our inner fire goes out. It is then burst into flame by an encounter with another human being. We should all be thankful for those people who rekindle the inner spirit. 99
>
> – Albert Schweitzer

ditional responsibilities, department structures would become convoluted, and frustration would spread.

I became fascinated by the art and mechanics of providing fair, useful feedback. When teaching communication early in my career, I would ask participants to brainstorm what the word "feedback" evoked in them. Invariably, they responded with "negative," "bad news," "criticism." We would then discuss techniques of how to deliver feedback. We'd talk about the need to balance "constructive" with "positive." They'd hear about providing feedback near the time of the other's behavior. Some techniques provided steps in the right direction, but felt mechanistic to me. Others seemed helpful but not sufficient. Something significant was missing.

Then one afternoon, from my office in a glass, steel, and marble environment, I watched a colleague walk down a long hall into our manager's office. I felt for the young woman; I knew she was about to be fired. She had been told for months her work performance was not adequate and had been counseled and coached about how to improve her methods and results. The news would surely be difficult for her, though it wouldn't come as a complete surprise.

An hour later, the colleague walked out of our manager's office, eyes red from crying, with a quiet smile on her face. Puzzled, I hurried to the manager's office to ask what she could have said to inspire a smile under the daunting circumstances. "I talked to her about her strengths, her favored work style, her personality when she was thriving," the manager said. "Then we contrasted those with the position she's been holding," she explained.

Witnessing the balanced firing inspired me. It sounded like an extended gardening metaphor, in which our manager helped the employee see that perhaps she wasn't planted in the right soil. And it stopped me in my tracks.

I had worked for years to toughen up when providing and receiving critical feedback. In my own management roles, at times I had practiced a negative way, learned in my upbringing, of delivering feedback. Looking back, I think the "stars" I managed enjoyed my style, but an employee who was seriously not measuring up must have dreaded a feedback discussion.

My manager's modeling led me to consider offering feedback in ways that might nourish the other's spirit. I began years of studying how to practice what I began to think of as "feeding back."

I've learned that, to offer inspiring feedback, we must use more than techniques and a slight shift in attitude. The art of feeding back requires that we carefully consider our own role in the communication. This is not an easy task; it requires learning to communicate bad news in ways that respect the integrity of the receiver.

Through the Nonviolent Communication model developed by Marshall Rosenberg, I'm learning to pause and prepare for a discussion, to examine my assumptions, to identify my own and others' needs, and to listen more deeply. In the Appreciative Inquiry process, championed by David Cooperrider, I'm reminded to look first at what an individual is doing right and to help them build on their strengths.

Feeding back, these days for me, means encouraging others to enlarge their range of behaviors and skills, rather than merely focusing on their flaws. As we examine an individual's weaknesses, we can talk about how any strength overextended will likely become a weakness. Together we can consider the realities and requirements of a particular assignment or role. We can discuss the larger context of culture, expectations, and what the individual needs to offer and receive in order to fulfill his/her role and begin to flourish.

When we view a person's skills on a continuum, from starting point to mastery, we hear less "I'm not creative," or "I'm not good with technology" and more "How can I develop?" Continuums remind us that seldom are we all good or all bad in behavior or even in work performance. Continuums can help us visualize opportunities to grow, spur us on in our development. I'm not yet at mastery in offering feedback, but I'm moving forward.

> 66 No matter what our attempts to inform, it is our ability to inspire that will turn the tides. 99 – Jan Phillips

Journey Questions

Parker Palmer writes: "A leader is someone with the power to project either shadow or light onto some part of the world and onto the lives of the people who dwell there." Through your own experience, what have you learned about feeding back?

How do you project light onto the lives of the people in your world?

Kathleen McSweeney is a leadership coach, photographer, and Chrysalis Council member. Kathleen is active in a writing group where members offer each other inspiring feedback and a book club where she experiences the richness a collaboration of voices can bring to any novel.

Synchronicity and Inner Guidance

by Nancy Bost Millner

B Millner

C. G. Jung is reported to have said "with my theory of synchronicity my thought hit the ceiling." Perhaps that statement can give people like me some consolation as we try to learn about this immensely important concept which seems to elude intellectual grasp.

Synchronicity has been defined as "meaningful coincidence." Synchronistic incidences occur unexpectedly and seem to be related neither by accident nor cause, but related by meaning. Another way of saying this is: in synchronicity, we experience the psychic and physical worlds coming together to offer us an invitation for personal and spiritual growth. Does the physical world respond with concrete

> " A synchronicity acts as an emergent event from an archetypal field in which the inner and outer world is experienced as a unity and as such felt to be spiritually meaningful. "
> – Angelo Spoto

reinforcement, allowing us to trust what we might find too difficult to believe from the psychic world alone?

It is the strong sense of meaning in coincidences that calls us to recognize their importance and call them synchronistic. It is in recognizing this sense of meaning that convinces many of us beyond doubt that there is a Reality greater than the physical one in which we move daily.

People experience such occurrences often, but it is said that only *journey people* recognize them. When one thinks of a person from one's past who has not been thought of for a decade and the person calls on the telephone that day, or when the dream image of a wounded crow is reinforced by the finding of a wounded crow on one's patio the next day, one may be experiencing synchronicity. And though all coincidences are not synchronistic (only meaningful ones), we in our materialistic culture might be at least advised to ask if there is a message in such happenings.

I recently experienced what I believe to be a synchronistic happening. After working on a dream with my dream group one member of the group suggested that I read a book titled *Creation Continues*, by Fritz Kunkel. The book is out of print, but I have had it in my book case for many years. The suggestion seemed on target with the dream and I rushed home to find the book directly in front of me, in the middle of the middle shelf of my bookcase. Later in the day, when I picked the mail from my mailbox, there was a brochure announcing a weekend study of *Creation Continues*. I checked my busy calendar, found it totally clear, wrote a check for the workshop and booked a flight to California. In several weeks I will attend the weekend. What do I expect? I'm not certain, but I am clear that I should go.

Synchronicity is important. It can connect us to our deeper selves, push us toward individuation and connect us with the Larger Story of which our small story may be a part.

As with everything, there are requirements for living a life in tune with synchronistic events. The most importance is awareness and a refusal to dismiss ambiguity, paradox or anything not immediately understood. Another is trust that there are forces beyond our conscious knowledge which have a benevolent interest in our well-being and the evolution of our culture. Yet another requirement is a trust in our ability to discern what actions are beneficial — or trust in our ability to correct our mistakes if need be.

We can only act on our best understanding, but we can often determine if we are on track by noticing the way in which our lives flow. A sense of ease, order, connection, peace and confidence in ourselves and our deeper knowing — sometimes called "absolute knowledge" — are good signs. We often fear what Jung calls "absolute knowledge," for we fear inflation or manipulation of others for our own selfish/egotistic reasons. Actually, the awareness of this possibility may provide some safety.

Absolute knowledge is actually knowledge beyond ego knowledge. It is inner truth confirmed by a willingness to act without assurance of self-reward or success. Absolute knowledge is not self-serving nor manipulative. Absolute knowledge, correctly discerned, can lead to the evolution of individuals and culture. Synchronicity may be its evidence.

66 Synchronicity is God wishing to remain anonymous. 99 – Anonymous

Journey Suggestions

For a month, track any synchronicities (meaningful coincidences) in your life.

Journal and/or share these and explore if they are providing meaning and/or guidance for your life.

If guidance is being offered, evaluate it and, if appropriate, act on it.

Nancy Bost Millner was the founder of The Chrysalis Group. She initiated the monthly *Words for the Journey* in 2004.

Acknowledgments

Words for the Journey has been an amazing Chrysalis community effort. We'd like to thank the following devoted Chrysalis friends:

Nancy Millner, Chrysalis founder, creator of and writer for Chrysalis's monthly *Words for the Journey* e-publication.

Our current President, Priscilla Burbank, whose energy and determination took a good idea and made it happen.

The Board of Directors of Chrysalis, whose leadership and support were essential.

All of our writers and artists, who shared their words, images and talents to create this collection.

Our Circle of Readers: Priscilla Burbank, Wilda Ferguson, Lenore Gay, Monchie Gibby, Kathleen McSweeney, Peggy Siegel, Janice Straub and Martha Tyler, who read and evaluated many entries and helped us to select the reflections included in this collection.

Margie Nea, who advised us on all artistic matters.

Adrian Luxmoore, who graciously consulted on all aspects of design and production.

And our patient, good-humored designer, Trina Lambert, whose artistry made it all so beautiful.

Liz Whitehurst
Susan Wilkes
Editors

History of Chrysalis

The Chrysalis Group, a nonprofit organization, was founded in 1994 by Nancy Bost Millner to provide the Richmond, Virginia, community with opportunities for psychological and spiritual growth. Her vision was "to provide hospitable time and space for seekers on diverse paths who wish to explore ways in which we can live connected to our true selves, to each other, to creation, and to The Spirit."

From those early beginnings, Chrysalis brought nationally known spiritual leaders such as Parker Palmer, Marcus Borg, James Hollis, Margaret Wheatley, Peter Russell and Tara Brach to Richmond to share their knowledge and expertise. Our permanent outdoor labyrinth allows open access for all who wish to experience the power of this ancient ritual. Over the years, thousands of people have attended innovative lectures, workshops, classes and spiritual practice groups which Chrysalis has offered for our membership and for the broader community.

Chrysalis is embarking on an exciting path in its ongoing journey, becoming The Chrysalis Institute in 2013. A vibrant resource and learning center for exploring insights and practices from the world's spiritual traditions, philosophies and contemporary scientific discoveries, its mission remains rooted in our founder's purpose: to encourage all seekers to spiritual growth and explorations beyond traditional boundaries.

Proceeds from the sale of this book support the Chrysalis mission. To become a member and receive the monthly *Words for the Journey* e-publication, to order books, or for more information about Chrysalis, please visit our website, www.thechrysalisgroup.com.

23493997R00053

Made in the USA
Charleston, SC
26 October 2013